D0853093

THE SUFFERING SERVANT

THE SUFFERING SERVANT

A Holy Week Exposition of Isaiah 52:13–53:12

Carlyle Marney

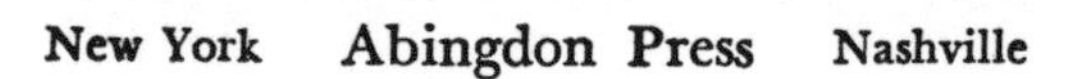

New York Abingdon Press Nashville

THE SUFFERING SERVANT

Library of Congress Catalog Card Number: 65-15234

SET UP, PRINTED, AND BOUND BY THE PARTHENON PRESS, AT NASHVILLE, TENNESSEE, UNITED STATES OF AMERICA

For the Holy Week Congregation

PREFACE

Not prepared for, or in anticipation of, their publication these Holy Week meditations for my own congregation have not been given elsewhere, and came rapidly, too rapidly, under the pressures of a daily delivery hour. Even though my early morning hours have given opportunity to cast a colder eye over them I have let them stand as they came out last spring as demonstrations of how much help a working pastor can get from a single book: *The Interpreter's Bible.* All technical materials came from Volume V of that splendid modern publication. I had no time to work elsewhere. The biblical text throughout is that of *The Bible, An American Translation,* published by the University of Chicago Press.

CARLYLE MARNEY

CONTENTS

Introductory 11

I. The Startling of the Nations
(Palm Sunday) 21

II. Who Could Have Believed It?
(Monday of Holy Week) 29

III. It Was Our Sickness
(Tuesday of Holy Week) 41

IV. All We Like Sheep
(Wednesday of Holy Week) 49

V. Dumb Before His Shearers
(Thursday of Holy Week) 59

VI. They Made His Grave
(Interlude for Maundy Thursday) . . . 71

VII. Through His Suffering Shall He See
(Good Friday) 77

VIII. Because He Interposed
(Easter Sunday) 87

INTRODUCTORY

Would you use this incredible poetry all this Holy Week without recalling its setting?

The word had gone out that that young man Cyrus from the East was a comer. He must be watched. His name already had a threatening effect upon any who seemed to stand in his way.

It was, says Toynbee, near the end of the Syrian "time of troubles." The old Semitic power centers were falling in on themselves. New hordes, whole armies, unknown peoples, began to appear on the great round stage which surrounded as an horizon the Fertile Crescent. Following the old Assyrians, Babylonians, and Egyptians in their tragic round came Medes, Persians, Greeks, and lesser peoples such as Israelites and their neighbors. Nothing in that ancient world would stay nailed down. Vast social movements hurled established history around. Bright armor and armies corroded and died. A new fear swept the stage wrapping itself in a new perplexity and a strange humility. The old power categories were no longer relevant. Everywhere men wanted something old, steady, permanent to feed their profound nostalgia for a past they had hated.

About seventy years before Cyrus the breakup began when Ashurbanipal, Emperor of Assyria, had died. Nabopolassar of Chaldea revolted. Cyaxares of Media revolted. And Herodotus says that for twenty-eight years the Scythian hordes overran Asia.

Egypt, under Psamtik I, was in one of her periodic upswings when, in 612 B.C., the Chaldeans and the Medes destroyed once-mighty Nineveh, capital of Ashurbanipal's Assyria. And thus it came that Pharaoh Necho came up to rescue the leftovers of the Assyrian armies besieged at Harran, and on the way disposed of Josiah, King of Judah, who tried, like a cock-partridge attacking a dog, to interfere at Megiddo. But all this was before the end of the world.

A new general—Nebuchadrezzar—came to meet the Egyptians at famed Carchemish and the neo-Babylonian empire was made. For forty-two brilliant years Nebuchadrezzar ruled from Babylon. Jehoiakim of Judah revolted, and the first captivity of the Jews began, in 597, with the son of the king among the prisoners for thirty-seven years in Babylon. Zedekiah reigned in Judah eleven years, rebelled in 588, but by 586 the Babylonians moved to take Jerusalem, blind Zedekiah, destroy the city, and burn the temple of Solomon. David's throne was emptied and his line ended forever.

It takes history awhile to kill off a Nebuchadrezzar. Amel-Marduk held up two years, then his son-in-law Nergalsharusur, then Labashi-Marduk; but Nabonidus, son of a woman kidnaped at Harran fifty-six years before, favorite wife of Nebuchadrezzar for about forty years, was waiting in the wings, and the conspirators enthroned him in 556.

Now Nabonidus had a hobby: he was a *theologian!* They seldom make good emperors. He rejected the god Marduk; he upheld Sin, the moon god (is he one of the Sabeans known to Maimonides?) ; he became fascinated with archaeology and retired to dig for old treasures in Edom.

Hence, Belshazzar, his son, was regent in Babylon, with his father three hundred miles away, when Cyrus came like a whirlwind out of the East. Up to now, the Medes had divided the world with Babylon, but Cyrus of Elam had rebelled and was joined by some Medes. He took Medea; he overwhelmed old Croesus (at Sardes), who thought he would not fight. He ran over the Phrygians, the Cappadocians, and the Arabs—then whirled on Babylon, and Nabonidus came home too late. The priests of Marduk had turned and said Marduk had turned—to Cyrus, so in October, 539, the anointed of Marduk took Babylon.

That famous Cyrus Cylinder reads like Second Isaiah: Babylon fell by the will of Marduk. Nabonidus has been judged. Marduk "scanned and looked" for a righteous man to lead him in the annual parades. He pronounced Cyrus ruler of the world. "He made him set out on the road to Babylon going at his side like a real friend."

Cyrus was something! The nations were startled.

Watching all this, sidelined by history, there was a community of faith in Babylon, a remnant from that Israel of seventy years before. The community included a young successor to the great Isaiah. Some say he could have been a sixth-century community teacher. We know neither his name, his father, nor his dates, but he was learning to read his own history for *deeds of Yahweh.* His works, some of them, were added to the oracles of the great Isaiah from two centuries before—but his poems soared beyond his master, and:

He became a voice incarnate in the preparing of the way of the Word. For him the Word dimmed all the Babylonian reality. The coming of the Lord transcended everything. God who is God would *do!* With profound inwardness, intimacy, and sensitivity, and his deep sense of divine reality at work in history, this Isaiah grasps the Jewish epic like none other before Paul. He has his firsthand knowledge of Babylon; he is an eyewitness to the making of idols; he watches the god-parades; he walks in Cyrus' train; he even writes poems to Cyrus—or adapts them. He is the grandest of all the prophets and Israel's most profound thinker. He was, says Martin Buber, "the originator of a theology of world-history."

He leaves us one fantastic poem of 199 strophes, with three major divisions—and its theme. Just as Cyrus has come to Babylon so God will come.

The work opens with the lone voice of a giant figure stumbling over the ruins of Jerusalem—

Comfort, comfort, speak comfortingly to Jerusalem!
Tell her that her warfare is done with
her iniquity is leveled out
She has received twice her weight for her sins.

And for 121 magnificent sets of lines, including proems and codas, there is not anything anywhere like it:

The Lord himself is coming, the Creator of the ends of the earth will put the nations on trial in a new assize event, a divine interruption, in which his blind and deaf Servant will see the redemption of Yahweh working, and Israel, led by grace through streams in the desert will just so see God's glory in her own desert and the emptiness of idol-making. The coming of the great Cyrus is a sign of this—there will follow the conversion of the nations, the collapse of other gods, the virgin of Babylon will be emptied of honor, and Israel's fulfillment is at hand through the Servant of the Lord who is called, sent, and comforted. Impenitent Israel, too, will confess the Servant in her coming experiences of salvatory grace and judgment, and, the Lord has become king. The Suffering Servant is the consolation of Israel and grace abounds.

Our concern for this Holy Week is with the 111th through the 115th strophes (Isa. 52:13–53:12):

The Sufferings and the Triumph of the Servant.

It has been called the most influential poem in any literature. And nowhere in the Old Testament is there to be found a more complete foreshadowing of the Christian gospel:

God, the Creator, the sovereign of all nations, is at work in the history of a sinful people through the judgment and redemption that characterizes his forgiveness. In preparation for the evangelizing of all mankind he is choosing, training, and empowering his servant church from among the unresponsive. A nation of sufferers will bring the peoples to repentance and for his own love's sake men will see the

Salvation of the World.

That the suffering of the righteous will bring redemption to many as an answer to all pain and grief is the basis of New Testament thinking. Here the church turned for its own explanation of the death of the Son of God. The poem opens with a dramatic dialogue—*Divina Commedia*—between God and the kings of the nations.

Palm Sunday

Lo! my servant shall prosper,
He shall be exalted, and lifted up, and shall be very high.
As many were amazed at him—
So marred was his appearance from that of a man,
And his form from that of the sons of men—
So shall he startle many nations,
On account of him kings shall shut their mouths;
For what has not been told them shall they see,
And what they have not heard shall they contemplate.

I

THE STARTLING OF THE NATIONS

Palm Sunday

Now what does it take to startle a nation? Before what event would a king shut his mouth? What event in the rush of events, what sight in a landscape, what sound in the cacophony of sounds will get a king's shut-mouthed attention?

Only some mighty contradiction of the expected course of things can do this. Some interruption, some diverting of forces, some conflagration or quaking or some collapse, you say. But this is not always so. After the public stands fell in at the games in Rome and fifty thousand died, Caligula (Little Boots), the Emperor, wished only that all Romans had one neck so that he could sever their head with one blow. The riot in the arena over a referee's decision in Lima last year which killed two hundred brought only a momentary *tsk! tsk!* about the foibles of the folk from any official source. The barest official expression of regret covered the death of six hundred on their way to work when in Tokyo Bay their ferry flipped over in a sudden tidal sweep.

Public disaster, freaks of the winds or waves, "acts of God," get only the momentary attention of the kings of the earth who have many another item of daily concern. But what brings the huge and shambling Emperor of the Franks or the dainty ageing patrician of the Abyssinians across thousands of miles to walk flat-footed in funeral parade? What commands a nation's stunned silence before an awful open grave? What lights a "perennial" torch in a graveyard and keeps the long lines standing for years? What can hold the riveted attention of men the world across for two thousand years in some concentration of concern and woe and hope?

A derringer shot in Ford's Theater can do it. The flat slap of a high-powered rifle can do it. The lifting of a cross has done it. Even a hangman's noose can do this. But not even these can hold our eyes for long unless their use involves the death of some young or fair or nobly intentioned man or people. How strange that not even the coronation of a Cyrus or a Charlemagne but only the murder of a Kennedy or the crucifixion of a young (they are always young) Messiah can get such shut-mouthed attention from the rulers of the earth. But you are right: it would have to be a contradiction. Something so shattering that it denies all our measurements and standards, our hopes and expectancies; only some such can shut-mouth kings and claim our long-spanned attention. Some event only that involves our fundamental symbols in some agonized contradiction can hold us across a century of remembered concern. This is why man and his emperors cluster around those corners where the young and the fair and the courageous, the dreamer idealists and prophets, the men who do not count costs and who pay a proper price for this luxury, are taken from us, with violence. It takes a contradiction.

Look at the poem! See that at which the kings of the earth are invited to gaze shut-mouthed.

> Look, he says, at the exaltation
> of my Servant
>
> This prudent dealer, this extolled one,
> He is very high.

Except that he is so messed up as to be unrecognizable as a man! And this was a startler to get the attention of kings. It was a mighty contradiction.

No wonder the church got in on the ownership of this poem. Nothing else in literature can so well explain his death. But it is ours only as it is first and still the property and the inheritance of Israel!

It is addressed to the nations. It is composed for the Israel of God. Here at last is an answer to Israel's despair and blindness. Here begins the third-act denouement within history of a mighty compelling theodicy. God will look good in history by what he *does* in a people. All the great Jewish motifs are present: here is the mission of Israel and here is the relation of Israel to the nations. And supremely, here is the concentrated essence of the meaning of Israel's hurting, and that final exulting exaltation.

> "My Servant," the wise-dealer, will prosper. His ultimate triumph is related to his wisdom. His task is to be the developer of the purposes of Yahweh. His relation to Yahweh guarantees that he knows the meaning of his sufferings,

and,

> You can tell he is somebody by the way the kings of the earth react.

The reversal of any death is a world-shaker, and Israel was dead. Who can come back from a death like Jerusalem's? Who can go home after seventy years in Babylon? What Lord can reign from a gibbet? What people can be slaughtered six million strong 2,500 years after they have been killed off? What cleverness of ours has been made absurd here? What incredible and divine sagacity is at work to confound our judgment that a process is *fini?* Can we never be sure when the play is over?

The poem promises some compelling self-disclosure of the Almighty. Is it that he will reign from the tree? Is it that the Lord will conquer from a colt? Or is this the symbol which participates in the incredible theodicy that all our history is a chance to witness?

He had been to hear some touted Rabbi from up East and had held his tongue through the long and unctuous representation of a Jewry turned hollow by its American captivity, but still thinking itself to be Israel. He had almost shouted out his shock at that point in the smooth address where the then kings of the earth had been blanketed in a bland and patronizing pardon for what they knew was going on in Europe, but about which they had done less than they knew. (He himself had wept in the corridors of power for the insignificant ransom to bring fifteen hundred Jews across the Bulgarian border when some of the political Israeli were turning their heads.) But now, at home in our place, he stalked the floor with four thousand years of the weight of oppression in his stride—short and thick and purpled with his scorn for that "Jew," such a *secular* Jew, such a pseudo Jew, such a prostitution of Judah; it came rushing out at last, as he tore at his flannel shirt in the old gesture of Jewish grief, at my wailing wall, he cried:

> Six million Jesuses! And they died like Jesuses! And what will Yahweh do with these!

The answer is the startling of the nations.

Monday of Holy Week

Who could have believed what we have heard?
And the might of the Lord—to whom has it been revealed?
For he grew up like a sapling before us,
Like a root out of dry ground;
He had no form nor charm, that we should look upon him,
No appearance that we should desire him.
He was despised, and avoided by men,
A man afflicted by pains, and familiar with sickness;
And like one from whom men hide their faces,
He was despised, and we took no account of him.

II

WHO COULD HAVE BELIEVED IT?

Monday of Holy Week

When God placards his doings in a poem it is always done dialogically. There is always room for human rejoinder. Before this God-advertised startler introduced in stanza 1 the shut-mouthed kings now open their mouths to say, "Who on earth could have believed it?" But they say it on the same stage, in the same setting, with the pronouncement of Yahweh which precedes it. The music does not descend to a lower pitch. It's a conversation between contemporaries—God and the kings of earth.

For that matter, the level of the whole movement is that of an impossible elevation. What singer can endure this *tessitura?* The range required of us is almost beyond our performance; it is like the choral finale of Beethoven's *Ninth Symphony*. For fifteen chapters (40-55) it goes. As James Muilenburg in his discussion of the servant poem expresses it: "Nowhere [is there] . . . a continuous series of poems by a single author of a range comparable to these chapters in Isaiah, with the possible exception of the book of Job."

But the kings can talk back. In the context of such an elevation of thought, intense lyricism, superb reflection of environment, sense of time; in an unprecedented God-centeredness, expressing so concretely the relation between Israel and God, with an imaginative insight unmatched until Paul or Augustine; the kings made a reply. Nor does their vocal entry bring a dropping, even temporarily, of major and exalted motifs. There carries through this persistence of concern over nations the promise of a return, the glorifying of Yahweh, the redemption of Israel, the covenant of the peoples, the overtones of Israel's despair centering in the Servant of the Lord. There is no decline of theme in the interlude which is the confession of kings. The pitch does not change.

They begin, "Who could have believed it?" And the reference is to yesterday's strophe, the content of which had shut their mouths. Who could have belived and anticipated that—

God's own prospering Servant
  would have been so marred as to seem inhuman?

That—

God's chosen people
  should be battered beyond identification?

There is a terrible contradiction at the root of things, they are saying back to God. But for that matter there are other demonstrations of the malady at the bottom of things.

Who could have anticipated that the "prince people" who had seen God's face through Jacob at Peniel would have gone "a whoring" after strange gods? Who could have foreseen that the temple of Solomon for the men of all nations should have become a pile of rubble before its time, or that the Holy City that would need no ark for a reminder would one day be infested with jackals? Who could have believed it? *"Isn't this just like God?"*

How odd
of God,
To choose
the Jews.

The startled kings recover their voices and confess that our history cannot be read without surprise—and isn't this just like God? We should have known all the time! Yet, who has ever understood how God works, they excuse themselves. For the problem is not only with God—it is with history too. History doesn't read right! It cannot be counted on at face value.

Take this "servant people" business, for example, they say. They grew up right before us, we saw them. They fought, suffered, sang, built, failed, sinned, endured, went captive, and died right before us. They were like an unplanted sapling. They were as unanticipated as a sprout out of dry ground. Is not this just like God to call this people his specialty? Or worse, even—*isn't this just like history?*

Start where you will: history simply makes no sense. The Emperor Constantine's mother, a barmaid in Gaul who slept with a Roman general passing through (that sallow general they called Constantius Chlorus, the green one); the reformer Martin Luther, the choirboy son of a German miner. Or go further back to find the vice-regent of Egypt, abandoned in a well; or mighty Moses, a foundling in a basket. Move around in our time: colossal Tom Wolfe comes from a stonecutter and a boardinghouse in Asheville; Abraham Lincoln follows an old cow onto an Ohio River raft at the end of a road in Kentucky. Or get current and see Martin Luther King on a day coach as a lad riding up to enlist for his own *Odyssey* at Crozer Seminary, where "What Chester makes makes Chester!" Isn't this just like history? Who could have believed it? Isn't it just like God? We should have known it all the while.

The early church had an agonizing problem with that scandal on its hands. How could the torture, disfigurement, and death of the Son of God be a part of their history without being so incongruous as to deny his very identity? But it was part of an older and larger problem.

How could the agony, disfigurement, and death of God's chosen people be their history without being so incongruous as to deny their identity? But this was part of a larger problem.

How can the agony, disfigurement, and death of all mankind be reconciled with our identity as made "in the image and likeness of God"?

It was the *agon* of all times and climes and peoples.

Who can give a meaning to our suffering? How can suffering be endured?

This is the contradiction in things that the poem will answer. Here the kings of the earth are called to see—the Suffering Servant! Isn't it just like God to make redemption everywhere an innocent or a good man suffers? Isn't it just like God to make salvation out of hurting?

The early church seized on this. Before long, one, so carried away with the love of God he was heretical about it, copied Hosea and said God suffers too! Isn't it just like God to suffer with us in the face of our freedom? But the heresy died down until it re-emerged as orthodox teaching, fifteen hundred years after that Patripassian (Father-suffering) extravagance of grace.

Mainly, the early church seized on and identified with him, the Servant Son. Like a sapling he grew up in Nazareth. Like a root we did not expect he broke through in Bethlehem in Judah. There was no charm, no form, no appearance to give us a clue. Indeed, there was everything to turn us away. So we took no account of him, the kings confess. Who could have expected us to believe that such a reversal was possible?

Yet, our own sickness should have told us. Our own history should have warned us. Our own memories of where God's men have come from should have taught us. We should never have overlooked the saplings; we must not tread down the sprouts; theirs is an amazing potential. We dare not mark off that despised suffering until we see what kind of redemption God is making.

This is the *lapsus theodicae* of all the so-called divine healers! They have missed the meaning of the suffering. They would teach us to run from and despise the means of the world's redemption. And who will comfort all those lamed, halted, blinded, and suffering ones who are always left behind when any "healer" has come and gone?

Most of these will not tell anyone who could help that they entertained their false high hopes for a healing. For days their hopes had built up—a miracle!—but now the healer has taken the offering and has gone on. Hopes torpedoed, faith twisted, those not healed have two alternatives:

They blame themselves for not having "enough" faith;
or they blame God for listening to some but not to others.

But there are better reasons:

Perhaps all the white cards that put you in the special line for those who cannot walk were gone already. Perhaps the pink or blue or green or yellow slips with the letter on them to identify your psychological "type" were given away. Perhaps there were not enough "counselors" to brief you for your confrontation with the Almighty. Or worse, perhaps you did get a card. You stood in line with all the other walking-wounded with your infirmity hanging over you. You waited and waited and waited until the "healer" was lifting his hand over you, but the smell of his ordinary sweat pinched your nostrils and your faith lay down and died, right there. And so the "healer" has gone, and you are left with a deep despair.

There are other maybes: even for those who resort to private "practitioners" in the old Victorian and carpeted haunts of the starry-eyed prayer-bands that linger on in every little village. Perhaps healing is a natural process governed by laws of nature. Or certainly—is it possible that there is *a meaning, depth, color, and power in suffering that we have missed if we run, frightened, from it?*

Perhaps you really are sick, not subject to cure by a "state of mind." Perhaps you are just not emotionally susceptible to suggestion; or perhaps, like myself, you really are skeptical. You worry some about the ranches, autos, downtown real estate, and Black Angus cattle that seem to pile up around these traveling healers. Perhaps, like myself, you find more reason to believe in God and your own suffering than you do in "healers."

This concerns a point the kings of the earth are confessing. We, too, have missed the meaning of the suffering. Isn't it just like God to take suffering and make it a means of redemption? It was my personal Apostle of Freedom, Nikolai Berdyaev, who first taught me that God keeps on doing this; that everywhere a good man suffers he releases redemption for the need that surrounds him—the watchers taste his redemption in the way he suffers. And I and you, we have the power to say whether our suffering is unto life or unto death. But we have no power not to suffer. Of this power even God has deprived himself. Who could have believed it?

Tuesday of Holy Week

Yet it was our sicknesses that he bore,
Our pains that he carried;
While we accounted him stricken,
Smitten by God, and humbled.
He was pierced for our transgressions,
He was crushed for our iniquities;
The chastisement of our welfare was upon him,
And through his stripes we were healed.

III

IT WAS OUR SICKNESS
Tuesday of Holy Week

Sheer genius—eight short lines on which float the two gigantic ideas without which there could be no Christian or Jewish faith!

Recognition; that is, *identification:*

It was our pain
Our sorrow

and *redemption:*

that he bore
that he carried.

Here is the distilled essence of Jewishness. No frame other than the poetic could carry the load of this impassioned drama. It is lofty, devastating music which only strings and reeds can carry. The music for brass and tympani comes later. The moment is intensely personal, but there is a cosmic backdrop—a vast panorama in which heaven and earth, past, present, and future, with Israel and Yahweh at the center, are the major figures. But this is not a drama that is channeled or structured. The parts are inchoate. There is action all over the stage, and all the players are onstage. The parts are *being* played; they do not close out or leave. We are all still there: God; the people; the event; the prophet; the Word.

Downstage, front and center, before this cosmic backdrop; focused, set up *there* (Dasein) we see—

the Sufferer

and the startled watcher cries, "My God, that's the same thing I've got!" It is *my* sickness that he has. This is *identification.* This is *the* religious miracle. The Sufferer holds a mirror. You peer down over his cot and see your own face! You walk down the corridor with the rolling litter. You touch his hand and your eyes meet, and the Sufferer on the frame is yourself. You pass the nurse in the hall with whom you waited out his dying in that shrinking room last night, and you speak, and a faint smile, but no more, you do not talk. Both of you know that part of you died last night, but you keep walking. Down the avenue of twisted spines, scrofulous wounds, rent torsos from the Sunday wrecks, you know and feel:

It is *our* sickness.

This is *the religious miracle:* to know and recognize the agony of the Sufferer as your own. This is identification. To identify with him and all the rest, knowing in your bones the truth of old Donne's, "If a clod be washed away by the sea, Europe is the less, . . . any man's death diminishes me."

Identification is the miracle. The words of the symptomatology leap out of the drama: *our* sicknesses, *our* pains, *our* chastisement, *our* transgressions, *our* iniquities. The verbs take on vibrant adjectival precision: he was *stricken;* he was *smitten;* he was *humbled;* he was *pierced;* he was *crushed;* they tumble down the chart fastened to the foot of the bed like a clinical description of a terminal disaster—and the name on the chart is mine! It was *our* sickness.

And the new word: *redemption.* Carried forward in the other column of the chart, opposite the entries for fever, pulse, pressure, liquids, symptoms, on the treatment and response side are some other verbal clauses—but let your eye fall first to the signature at the bottom. The physician is—incredible—the Lord the Creator-Redeemer.

All the preceding strophes, 112 of them, lead into and demand the signature of Yahweh. Israel the Sufferer is forever under the treatment and care of her Holy Healer Lord. At Sinai she had become a holy people through God's grace-ful initiation and her answer of obedience. Earlier, at the Exodus, she had begun to taste her redemption. The cry was then and now:

I am the Lord who brought you up out of Egypt!

Now this symptomatology, this clinical description of the Sufferer's woes, is written under the expectancy of a tremendous *event*. The Healer himself will come on the floor. Israel's time of hurting is at an end. The old agony is passing away. A decisive end of the convulsion is at hand. Cyrus is but a flag announcing it. The new Exodus is a new healing. The new Covenant is pure grace involving a new wellness, wholeness, a new creation! The Healer comes! And this is theophanic language. Our God appears to us! As *Redeemer* who is *Creator* who is in our *history*. Healing, the central business of God which he does in his appearing on our ward, is an aspect of his creation-redemption which now puts forward the claim that the arm of Yahweh comforts, forgives, helps. *He* will release us from our bondage; he will deal wrathfully with our enemies; he will return us to Palestine; he will rebuild the Holy City; he will restore the land; yes, *he* will heal all the nations.

This is new. All healing is by theophany. Our God has come!

And so it is that on the treatment side of the chart, opposite the symptoms of pain, chastisement, transgression, and iniquity, there appear the initialed verbals of our treatment:

it was our sickness—*that he bore*
our pain—*that he carried*
our chastisement—*was upon him*
for our transgressions—*he was pierced*
for our iniquities—*he was crushed*

and we were healed.

That he bore; that he carried; we were healed! But I have a question, Doctor God. If I am healed why do not my symptoms go away?

Of course there is no wrong in our wishing to be well, but it is dreadfully wrong to so wish to be well that one depends upon the wrong source for healing and so misses the meaning of his hurting. Behind every "healer's" campaign and on the fringes of all the "healing circles-of-prayer" there are those whose hearts have been split with false hopes and missed meaning. The Christian faith speaks as much of healing as it does of teaching, but it points always to a Healer who has come. His healing, by whatever means the processes of our disintegration are temporarily reversed, points always to the disclosure of God in our lives for which we were made. And my symptoms which remain are an inoculation of *identification* which sustains me in that suffering business of becoming a redeemer-healer, too.

Wednesday of Holy Week

All we like sheep *had gone astray,*
We had turned everyone to his own way;
And the Lord made to light upon him
The guilt of us all.

IV

ALL WE LIKE SHEEP

Wednesday of Holy Week

The only name mentioned in the entire poem is here: The Lord has laid on him the iniquity of us all. But look at the pronouns all over the place:

> him, his, his, he, their, him, them,
> they, they, they, we, whom, he, him,
> he, we, him, we, him, he, their, he,
> we, he, our, our, we, he, our, he, our,
> him, us, his, we, we, we, his, him.

Is this use of pronouns deliberate? Is it just mere genius? And midway in the section that sweeping inclusive compelling *kullānû—of us all!* Then after this break the march of the pronouns continues:

> he, he, he, his, he, his, he, his, he, they,
> his, his, he, his, him, he, he, he, he, his,
> he, his, his, he, their, I, him, he, he, his.

That incredible pronoun *kullānû* tempts us first. *All of us; of us all,* yes. All of us watchers are involved, but look at the forty-six uses of the third person pronoun *he,* or *his,* or *him.* Who is this *he?*

If the Servant songs in the preceding chapters are the work of Second Isaiah as an integral part of his poem (and Muilenburg says the problems of dropping them are greater than of keeping them), then the Servant of the Lord is "certainly" Israel. But the *he* in the songs contrasts sharply with the portrait of the *he* in this poem, according to Johann Fischer, the Roman Catholic scholar:

> Above all in the supreme poem of the collection (52:13–53:12) the lines sketch the life story of an individual sufferer. There in a concreteness of detail . . . such a striking resemblance to an actual person that a collective entity like Israel seems out of the question. [Also] . . . the figure of the songs seems to stand in sharp contrast to the figure of the holy community of Israel.

The Servant Israel is despondent, fainthearted, admonished again and again to trust in God. *The Servant of Yahweh* overcomes any momentary despair through an unshakable trust in God. Israel is a sinner from birth. The Servant is guiltless because sinless. Israel suffers in discouraged exile for his own sins. The Servant suffers patiently, voluntarily, while interceding on behalf of others who sin. Israel suffers unwillingly, praying for vengeance against his enemies. The Servant suffers for Israel, cannot be identified with Israel, has an active mission to "bring Jacob back" that Israel might be gathered.

Fischer's contrasts are *too* clean. Israel is not just disobedient and scattered. Perhaps, says Muilenburg, instead of asking "Who is the Servant?" we ought to be asking "Who is Israel?" And on this line of inquiry Israel is *two*.

Israel is a wandering Aramaean whom the Lord with a strong arm brought up out of Egypt; but Israel is also a desert nomad gone a whoring in the wilderness with strange gods. Israel is the people-of-a-covenant with Yahweh the God of Israel and Israel the people of Yahweh; but Israel is also abandoned like a hut in a cucumber patch because of his moral leprosy. Israel is the community of faith on an Exodus led by Yahweh into a land of milk and honey; but Israel has committed adultery in the sacred groves under the trees of the Baalim. Israel is the community of Torah, Temple, Talmud, and *Shema:*

> Hear, O Israel, the Lord our God is One
> and thou shalt love. . . .

But Israel has loved too many too well, and his possessions are spilt and split from Dan to Babylon. Israel is the child of Abraham, Isaac, and Jacob, living in tents before Yahweh. Israel takes on as a social group the character of Abraham, and an intense presentation of this people as a single suffering man is "a normal Semitic way of speaking." Israel is captive, burning, leprous, and lost; Israel is also "God's own people"—God's darling, David; Israel is Rose of Sharon; but Israel is also treading the grapes of God's wrath in the winepresses of Gibeon. Israel is many! Israel is slave in Egypt, captive in Babylon, tortured in Spain, burned alive in York, ghettoed by his exclusivism and subjectivization of Torah in Warsaw. Israel is, says Sam, six million Jesuses dying like Jesuses while presidents and potentates and chairmen turn their heads. Israel is servant, and Israel alone is able to bear all that is said of the Servant of the Lord.

Who is this forty-six-times-named he or his or him? Here the poetic genius uses all of his material to picture the essence of the destiny of a servant people. As the people of Israel fulfill their own Covenant, the literature of the Old Testament isolates and withdraws them into suffering heaps of death and ruin. Who is this suffering *he*? He is Israel! God's anointed and impoverished. My God, how Israel has paid for his label—God's own people!

But the Jews as the Suffering Servant are a people *with a mirror*. The nations bend over the Sufferer's pallet and see their own face there reflected: it *was* our sickness. The lamenting confession of the nations continues amidst that torrent of personal pronouns. The Servant says no word at all. He is intensely present, never speaking. In short lines, powerful clauses, we are gripped by the swinging contrasts from humiliation and suffering to exaltation and triumph—between the many and the solitary—between then and now—between him, he and we, us—and then that incredibly inclusive Hebrew construct *kullānû*—

all of us—
of us all.

All we like sheep—like sheep we watch, like sheep we wander, like sheep we have no initiative, like sheep we cluster and wait, like sheep we scatter, like sheep we bear no responsibility—

And the Lord made to light upon him—the Lord has laid on the Servant people, the shepherd people, the responsible competent covenant people, the community of revelation and faith—the guilt of *kullānû* —of us all!

And pray, upon whom does the guilt of the whole now lie? Who knows better and obeys least? Who is captive in a thousand Babylons? Who keeps denying her brethren in vanity and pride and walks with swinging-hipped arrogance past the suffering innocent and the deprived? And who is now threatened with the loss of everything meaningful? All of us—of us all, within the church of the Lord, the covenant community. The people of the Talmud were one fulfilling of the Old Testament literature. There is another fulfilling for Torah—the Christ of God and the church of Christ. We have not finished with "Who is the Servant?"

From here one thing is very sure. Before our eyes the agonies that make a ghetto for Talmud and a cross for Christ continue unabatingly in power. And God's people, all of us who know better, have a responsibleness we have not seized.

Sing, O barren who has no offspring
Cry aloud you who know no pregnancy
For more are the children of desolation
Than the children of legitimacy.

And God has never liked for there to be so many children of desolation—even in Appalachia, much less the cities of the plain. And God, a judging God, has focused, has laid on a responsible people the guilt of us all.

Thursday of Holy Week

When he was oppressed, he humbled him-
self,
And opened not his mouth;
Like a sheep that is led to the slaughter,
Or like a ewe that is dumb before her shear-
ers,
He opened not his mouth.
Through violence in judgment was he taken
away,
And who gave thought to his fate—
How he was cut off from the land of the liv-
ing,
For our transgressions he was stricken to
death?

V

DUMB BEFORE HIS SHEARERS
Thursday of Holy Week

Who, then, is the Servant of the Lord? Israel, the church, some person? This is the "most exercised" Old Testament problem. Clearly the Servant is Israel in chapters 41, 43, 44, 45 and 48. Just as clearly the Servant is not Israel in chapters 42, 49, 50, 52, and 53. Who is the Servant, some individual?

He was, said Duhm, a prophet-teacher of the fifth century B.C., probably dying with leprosy. Mowinckel thinks him to have been a contemporary whose work was in the present—a Jew and a prophet, Second Isaiah himself. One famous student said in 1898 the

Servant was Zerubbabel, in 1901 he changed to Jehoiachin, in 1922 to Moses, and then in 1930 he decided it was the prophet but the fourth stanza—a funeral dirge—had been written by another, a Third Isaiah.

The list is longer. By some really competent teacher virtually everybody who was ever anybody to Israel has been nominated: Uzziah, Hezekiah, Josiah, Isaiah, a martyr of Manasseh's time, Jeremiah, Meshullam, the son of Zerubbabel, Eleazar the Maccabee. Every nominee has been rejected by all the scholars except his nominator! What does this confusion mean? Muilenburg says,

> [It means] no single person is sufficient to bear the burden of what is disclosed. . . . It is not such as any historical Israelite could be expected to accomplish; the scope [of the Mission] is wider than that of Jeremiah. The response (to an individual) expected of the Nation is too extraordinary. The described sufferings are too much for one.

Karl Budde has said: The usual identifications are "nothing short of fantastic, and the extreme of absurdity."

Yet, the fact remains that one fulfillment of the Old Testament rests squarely upon Isaiah's eschatological poems. The New Testament rises upon a base of the poems. The Gospel accounts of Jesus are impossible apart from an understanding of the writers' regard for these poems!

The earliest Gospel opens with a quote from the poems of Second Isaiah and sees Isaiah's matter fulfilled in the preaching of John the Baptizer. (Mark 1:1-3.)

Matthew and Luke reshape Isaiah 40 in their own ways. (Matthew 3:1-3; Luke 3:1-6.)

John's Gospel makes even more noteworthy use of the Isaiah material. (John 1:19-23.)

The hymns of the infancy in Luke are from Isaiah. (Luke 1:51-52, 54-55, 76-77; 2:30-32.) The words at the baptism of Jesus are Isaiah's. (Mark 1:11 and parallels.) Jesus quotes from Isaiah 61 in the synagogue scene. (Luke 4:16-18.)

Matthew explains the miracles as a fulfillment of Isaiah 42:1-4. In their accounts of the Transfiguration Mark, Matthew, and Luke all quote Isaiah 42:1. There is an "unmistakable allusion" to Isaiah 53 in Mark 10:45 ("For the Son of Man also came not to be served, but to serve, and to give his life a ransom for many." RSV) . In Luke 22:37 ("This scripture must be fulfilled in me, 'And he was reckoned with transgressors' "; RSV.) , in and under *all* the Gospels, and in the primary tradition received by Paul and expressed in I Corinthians 15:3, the Suffering Servant is present. Remember too the confrontation of the Isaiah 53 material in Philip's conversation with the royal Ethiopian (Acts 8:26-39).

Says Millar Burrows, "From Acts on the identification of Jesus with the Suffering Servant of the Lord is constant in the New Testament." H. Wheeler Robinson says, "[Without exaggeration] this is the most original and daring of all the characteristic features of the teaching of Jesus." This is it. It is settled. Torah misses the point. The New Testament is correct. The Servant is Messiah, the Christ of God.

But wait. If this is so, Jesus must have known it and talked about it, even taught it. If he knew who he was at all, he must have seen this. The way the student Jesus had poured over Isaiah he simply could not have missed this! And yet, not a single reference we have used contains a single indication even remotely in Jesus' own words that claims this. If he is the Suffering Servant of Isaiah, how could he have missed it? The whole New Testament mind walks right into this material, memorizes it, writes the confessional histories and composes hymns out of it, saying everywhere,

This is he.

Why did not Jesus say it—if he in fact did not? John Knox concludes that Jesus did not so regard himself, and the passages from Isaiah are certainly not Messianic in any accepted sense of the word.

Did Jesus not know this Suffering Servant set of poems? He seemed to know all the rest of Isaiah. Did Jesus not connect this Sufferer with Messiah? He seemed to know he must die. Did Jesus truly know who he was?

Somehow I cannot see Jesus of Nazareth bent over in the usual adolescent crisis about Who am I. There are two tremendous historical figures who seem to have leapt over that agonized Who am I. Only in a time of terrible stress did Moses' own identity become a problem to Moses. He *knew* to whom the Exodus belonged; and he knew whose the people were. He knew they all were Yahweh's. Yahweh was so *all* that Moses hardly matters to Moses. It's no question. And the Christ? Was there ever a human being more totally obsessed with who God is? This is the meaning of self-denial: the Who am I question no longer arises. The self has been utterly transcended in obedience to the Father!

It was so with Jesus: he shushed the disciples; he shrank from the name; if he asked, "Whom do men say that I am?" it was for a greater concern than the settling of his own identity to himself. It really was not a question that arose from his own concern in the light of his clear obsession with the Father. There must be a stronger reason why Jesus did not connect himself verbally (if he did not) with the Suffering Servant.

Look. The answer lies not in the New Testament but in the poem. Look at the character of the Servant. It is here a dramatic dialogue and the speaker is not God; it is the royal onlookers who use this confessional language. The *watchers* describe him; not the Sufferer or God.

Look again to the Servant: he humbled himself, he opened not his mouth, like a sheep, dumb before the shearers, no deceit in his mouth; he poured out; he bore;

and he never said a mumbling word!

The character of the Sufferer does not permit a self-identification by Jesus! He would have been out of character to say his own name.

The earlier poems had said he would be this way. The Servant says nothing—ever. The classic triad utterly silences the Servant:

He will not cry or lift up his voice,
or make it heard in the street (Isa. 42:2 RSV).

And the reason neither the Servant nor Christ says *any*thing? This is not a mere colossal modesty; nor a doubt or ignorance about his identity; nor an interpretation problem about Messiah. The silence is for the same reason that the Jews themselves have made so little use of the Servant poems.

For the Suffering Servant concept to be self-applied to a single man *or* a single people would require such daring, such implicit arrogant confidence, that "who could assume it?" becomes *the* revelant question. Who could claim *this* designation for himself? Only a twisted megalomania resting on some masochistic paranoia could say *this* is me. Symbols of this size can never be assumed by self-nomination! Not so it sticks for two thousand years!

Only another can say, "This is he!" Only from outside can the designation be made. Symbols of this proportion must be acknowledged from elsewhere!

Does Everest say, "I am the grandest, highest, and steepest?" Does Matterhorn name itself? Does Grand Canyon need a banner to tell the traveler he has arrived at its edge? Only a Cassius Clay says, "I'm the greatest!" (And that old Kentucky Cassius for whom he was named would never have bothered to say it.)

Not even Muhammad (whose name Cassius has taken) would say he was the greatest. Only some *other* can say who you are.

Who put this name on Christ? Who did this to the Suffering Servant? Well,

who watched Christ die—who saw his resurrection appearances—who read their own history, wrote their own books—and their confessions—and their hymns —and their theology on the identification of their Christ with the Suffering Servant of Israel?

The whole confessing, believing, participating Christian communion of all time—that's who! They are the only ones who *could* have done this. The *church* did it; it said and says, Look! There he is! Thou Christ!

C. F. D. Moule says that his person and work *were* redemptive; not necessarily his quotes. The early church saw this and recognized the Servant, and here we are. It is he. There is no other. In the redemption he *does,* in the memories he invokes, in the expectations he arouses, in the responsible obedience he demonstrates, in the Covenant he fulfills, in the universal manhood he personifies, in the Suffering Servant he *is* the salvation he *effects!*

Thou—He!

Faith says:

Thou dumb and fragile breaking suffering
He before thy shearers,
We know thee who thou art!

Interlude for Maundy Thursday

They made his grave *with the wicked,*
His tomb with evildoers;
Although he had done no violence,
Nor was any deceit in his mouth.

VI

THEY MADE HIS GRAVE

Interlude for Maundy Thursday

On Boot Hill outside old Virginia City, Montana, there are five graves in a row; graves of men hanged the same hour by Vigilantes from the rafters of an half-finished house. These five are a few of the more than thirty dealt with thus summarily by a self-appointed Citizens' Committee determined to stop the vicious slaughter of lonely travelers from the mines nearby. All five graves bear just-alike markers—name, date—except that one has a word not on the others.

It reads:

Haze Lyons
Hanged
Jan 14
1864

Peccavi

"I have sinned!" Who is this Haze Lyons hanged a hundred years ago, and what did he mean "I have sinned"? I do not know, and it made no difference. "They" hanged him anyway and "they" made his grave with the wicked, repent or not. He was buried, they say, with his kind.

And aren't we all? This is why the Roman Catholic Church and fraternal orders and burial associations are so careful about who goes in their private graves! A man is buried with his kind. Aren't we all?

It is so with the Suffering Servant, except here is the point. "They" with whom he was buried—they were *not* his kind. They were *our* kind. Incredible! In his grave at the ending of his road the Servant of Yahweh is united with us.

Once more there are pronouns all over the place. Who are the "they" who made his grave? In God's name how can the Roman Catholic (or any other) Church say who did not make his grave when we Jews in fact did make his grave, and when we cannot be rid of this even by not being Jews? The problem after two thousand years is for us all to be or not be Jews—not for us to be guiltless. Can a dead Roman constabulary bear *this* guilt? No more than a Mecklenburg County deputy sheriff can bear it! We Jews looking on, *we* made his grave with our own kind on the night he was betrayed. The "they" is impossible—it was a "we" who made his grave—else how can it ever be a grave made *for* us?

It is in the context of this grave we made, opening before us, too, that "we" who were "they" are now invited to drink our terrible toast to the death we have already witnessed in our baptism.

Come, then, all you who do truly love the Lord Jesus and are in amity and concord with your brethren, and let us break bread, and drink wine, and praise God, together, on our knees.

Good Friday

Yet the Lord was pleased to crush him by
sickness,
That when he made himself a guilt-offering,
He might see posterity, might prolong his life,
And the pleasure of the Lord might prosper
in his hand.
Now through his suffering shall he see it, *and*
be satisfied;
Through his affliction shall my servant, the
Righteous One,
bring righteousness to many,
And shall carry the burden of their guilt.
Therefore will I divide him a portion with
the great . . .

VII

THROUGH HIS SUFFERING SHALL HE SEE

Good Friday

This poetic drama that has occupied these days could have been much simpler if only it had come equipped with stage directions and role labels—like modern drama. Yet, in fact, there are such directions and labels in the drama. They are only more delicately given.

In most Hebrew poetry, it seems to me, the great words are the verbs, then the verbal adjectives, then the nouns to give the action and the situation their worth. In this poem these parts of speech move, writhe, and pound in a picture of unrelieved and excruciating suffering. They cannot be forgotten; they sear the mind:

> marred, startled, shut-mouthed,
> formless, charmless, despised, avoided,
> afflicted, stricken, smitten,
> humbled, pierced, crushed, oppressed,
> dumb, stricken to death,
> lifeblood poured out, numbered with transgressors,
> bore the sins of many,
> grave with the wicked.
> Like a sapling, like a root, like a sheep,
> Striped, sickened, afflicted by pains and dead.

But moving as they may be, the *key words* are still the pronouns which point up that fantastic contrast between he, him and we, us, with that vague "they" in between. Dozens of pronouns keep the action shifting back and forth—God and the nations; the Sufferer and the kings of the earth; him and us—and running throughout, that moving Hebrew construct *kullānû,* all of us.

Yet the great power of the pronouns in the poem is

not just contrast. Their real purpose is for *stage directions.* They shift the gaze. They are the prompters. They are the signposts and the role-labelers. They tell us where to look, between him and they and he and us, and the moving all we—all of us. *These bring the drama out into the orchestra and mezzanine. Suddenly we are all onstage caught up in the performance.* And now comes the denouement.

The Sufferer is at climax of the suffering. The grave has become a desirable end and his only refuge. The cool corridors of Sheol offer his only hope for succor and rest. The problem on stage, down front and center, is suffering: tortured, twisted, endless suffering; the suffering of the innocent kind; the not-guilty suffering; the more-than-Job suffering because here no friend can make it look good by imputing guilt. This is the suffering of the exquisitely innocent. This is lamb-suffering; this is child-suffering; suffering without cause in the sufferer.

Before this kind of suffering every great novel, drama, epic, and art form has been estopped. None has given us answer to "Why the suffering innocent?" —"Why are the children of the desolate always so many more than the children of the marriage?"

The incredible Hebrew genius has an answer! *It will change the pronoun!* The most important shift in the play is unheralded and unannounced. The Sufferer writhes before the grave—and the poem shifts its pronoun. The he, our, we, his, they of the drama become here in unprecedented effect the simple first personal pronoun, *I!* Yahweh speaks! And this is sheer genius; the keenest stroke in Second Isaiah's thirty chapters is this little shift from *he* to *I*. To this situation so startling as to shut the mouths of kings only Yahweh can speak, and it is sheer Hebraic genius of the first order accomplished with the little shift from *he* to *I*.

In *Green Pastures* De Lawd comes onstage at this point in magnificent portraiture to talk to the sufferer Hezdrel, but there is less stage business here in the poem. There is no shift in staging, no italicized directions for actors or chorus or orchestra. No introductions by a voice choir, no props, no sound background—it just shifts from he, his, to that incredible Hebrew

"*My* servant, . . . Therefore will *I* . . . ."

And it is like a lifted hand that could stop a convulsion. The spoken "my servant" stops the writhing. The "therefore will I" makes it almost all right, and this is the essence of the Jewish religious consciousness. This is radical monotheism at its crown and center. This is the very heart-belt of Jewish faith: the suffering of the innocent is under the eye and in the hands of Yahweh, who has his purpose for it.

Hear, O Israel, the Lord our God is One.

There is not a god for good and another for evil. They had no demons, as did the Greeks, for evil powers. There was not a god of the myrtle and another of the maple. There is no god you can make; no other god to split the load; there is no other God period! Whatever the agony or the contradiction God is One; all is caught up in him.

The Jews had no real need for Satan and no use for him. Satan is Persian, he is Satanas, the adversary. There is no Satan except myself in native Jewish thought. In the writings of Moses Maimonides both the serpent and Eve's tempting are *in Adam,* part of the man! The Jews had no Ahriman, God of the dark, no king of evil spirits with a domain of his own. Only post-Babylon does Satan appear on stage in Job or in certain late passages in Isaiah, and even here he, Satan, is still on conversational terms with God as an amiable sycophant and court hanger-on. The hint of Lucifer, fallen Star of the Morning, is Persian and very late coming to Judah.

Christians made much more use of Satan. Demons

were *in* by New Testament times, and Satanas, the adversary, the personification of a domain of darkness and evil, is a power to be overcome. But this represents an intrusion. Native Jewishness is monotheistic. In Jewish thought one does not explain his evil *or* his suffering by blaming a demigod. There is no other power, no other god, no incipient dualism. The sufferer in Job is *guilty,* they said, in order to preserve the justice of God; but even *innocent*—if he is—he is under the eye and hand of Yahweh.

This depth of innocent-suffering is not reached in Job or in Hosea, and it is never reached again from this poem on until at Golgotha, at edge of dark before the maw of the tomb, with Calvary dripping down his thighs and off his feet, tendons torn and writhing like coils of wire under the skin, he, the Sufferer Son cries:

> Father! Into *thy* hands I give over my breath!

And what an incredible use of a pronoun!

And what an accumulation in the poem of Hebrew genius. God had been onstage all the time. In the poem in chapter 40—hours ago—he had announced his decision: the way would be prepared by responsible people; a new event, a new Exodus was to be anticipated for which these responsible forerunners were to prepare the rough, smooth the bad, and raise the road in the valleys. An even more marvelous redemption than the old Exodus would be approaching in a new theophany. Here God's glory would be showing in such a universal that "all flesh shall see it together!" This means a changing of nature, a collecting of nations under divine sovereignty, and the inauguration of the kingdom of God. It is imminent—before our very eyes the first and last are tied together. And *all* this hangs on the major characteristics of the Hebrew religious mentality: they *remember*—and they *expect*—and this is as true to Isaiah as it is to Paul or Augustine (see his *Confessions*) or to modern eschatological hope.

Here the little shift, the tiny shift of a pronoun, puts God himself onstage at the center of innocent-suffering, and with what they remember and in the light of what they expect they see in the present a terrible suffering made into a full-orbed and glorious redemption.

Everything happens from the viewpoint of what God has begun, is fulfilling, and will end. And here all the darkness onstage is caught up in a revelation.

The revelation? That the way of suffering is a way to *see*. To remember means that the guilt, need, sin, and despair from Egypt on are of the realm of the *many,* and to expect means that God the One has the many *and* the innocent in his hands, and under his purpose a redemption is being made.

With utter comprehension of this moment in the drama the church wrote its memories of the death of the Son, and brings him at the last to the same setting in the same drama where he too shifts a pronoun and cries,

Father, into *thy* hands. . . .

And here John's Gospel adds a word: *It is finished!* And from here, on Good Friday, it *is* finished. The rest of the drama is God's.

Easter Sunday

And with the strong shall he share the spoil;
Because he poured out his lifeblood,
And was numbered with transgressors,
While he bore the sin of many,
And for transgressors he interposed.

VIII

BECAUSE HE INTERPOSED

Easter Sunday

In all the world is there any grace quite like that grace which takes on itself another's guilt? There is, of course, pity—which may be largely a reaction to contrast. There is mercy—the refusal to use an advantage to hurt, or the use of one's resources to help. There is love—which goes to meet a need and shares it. And then, there is *this* grace; the grace that takes on one's self the entire load of the other. The poem closes on a grace note—"and for transgressors he interposed." He intercedes. That is, he *becomes* the intercession.

In spite of all our intercessory praying there is no intercession without this: the pray-er becomes an intercession. He *is* the victim, sinner, needer, despairer. God is no lackey whom one can send to deliver a basket of blessing. The intercessor is on duty! (It has been twenty years since I have asked *God* to fix race relations in the South, for example. He has a clear majority down here if only we were intercessors too.) The poem reveals this principle of identification through the use of strong poignant verbs: *he bore the sin; he poured out* his lifeblood; *he carried* the burden of their guilt; *he brings* righteousness to many; *he makes himself* a guilt-offering for us; but mostly it says *he was numbered with the transgressors,*

and for transgressors he interposed.

He found that to do any good for transgressors with his life he had to get in the lineup!

Very thin now, twenty pounds too light, traveling in a sweat shirt and slacks with one tiny suitcase, she had called us from the bus station. We kept her three days to try to put a little strength in her. I kept remembering her fresh little-girl loveliness as a freshman in Texas, and had seen her graduation in Carolina. From the time she was six years old the only name we had used for her was a pet name, "G." She was enroute to Atlanta, then Jackson. She shuttles back and forth in the underground student drives to see a racial redemption in our time. We heard later she was jailed in Jackson for the third time, and I remember what her mother had wanted for her and that she had given her everything the magnolias at their best could bring—everything you want for yours—but G had spurned it for slacks and a bus and mimeograph ink and tired feet and the disinfected odor of town jails—to be numbered *with* the transgressors. Somewhere along the road she convinced her father that she had to be interposing her frail body where the transgressors are. It cost him his distinguished pastorate, a thirty-year prestige career in his denomination, and a three-thousand-mile removal to a community church, for he could not let her do *his* preaching. He had to be numbered with her—and with transgressors. On my desk today is her full-page article in the San Francisco *Chronicle* (her college graduation picture at the corner), her byline in big bold letters, for she writes like an angel with a scalpel; and a minor story on the side that her father had been knocking on the doors of his seminary classmates this long hot summer in Mississippi only to hear them say, "We do not interfere in these purely political matters!"

Or hear another, closer home. Three summers ago she was Queen of Lake Junaluska's festival, a proper and gracious product of a properly committed Methodist home on this very street where I preach. You can see her house when the sanctuary doors are opened after benediction. Her case comes up in a Carolina court next month. She found she had to number herself with transgressors.

Proper parents properly are perturbed when their youngsters take a gospel of identification with anything like proper seriousness. It puts them in strange corps in far places. And I, too, was shaken when a Methodist pastor wrote me that a boy whose name I don't even know had been carried off in Nashville's paddy wagon with a bloodied copy of my book on prejudice under his arm. Had I meant him to take me *that* seriously?

There is no redemption that can come from our uninvolvedness. Who can be saved by telephone? No drownings are stopped from the dock. I learned that before I was fifteen years old. One has to go in the deep to save. The redeemer is *always* numbered with the transgressors. Father Damien has to live *with* his lepers. The Savior can always be identified with those he saves. It is the last great theme of the poem; the

Suffering Servant has become one with those he aims to save. And God—the last speaker in the drama—simply cannot let this go by.

This is why the pronoun switches from *he, him,* to *my, I.* This is why God says:

Therefore will I divide him a portion with the great, and with the strong shall he share the spoil.

A portion with the great! God cannot be God and let this willingness to be numbered with the transgressors go unnoted: the really great among us have always been so numbered. "I will divide him a portion with the great." Was ever a promise better kept?

Resurrection is an earnest on the investment of all who ever numbered themselves with transgressors for the transgressor's sake. It is for all those

"... numberless unknown heroes
equal to the greatest heroes known!"

This is what resurrection is about. It is not a gratuity for everybody. It is not a given immortality and not a universal experience, I think. It is, rather, that God can be counted on to set the record straight. Those who number themselves with transgressors, those who interpose themselves for the sufferings of the world, are not left out of the great. God backs them up. There are situations of deprivation, suffering, and death that only a resurrection *can* atone. And the Cross, which said on Friday that there are things you can never pass, now gives way on Easter Sunday to an opened tomb which says a man can pass anything life imposes.

There are at least six, and likely eight, traditions of resurrection that the New Testament carries forward. Their origins lie in the memories of the ancient local fellowships of encounter with the Christ of God. Paul assesses and repeats them in the verifying of his own encounter with Christ Risen and makes this point:

If Christ be *not* risen we have no good news. If death is really the catchall that it is, then there is no way off this island unless God is God. If God is God there is a way away. If he is God he has to back his Servant.

Only the most twisted kind of wrong exegesis could put a doctrine of resurrection in Second Isaiah's poem. The promise there is an open promise, but not in the thought of personal resurrection at that time and in this poem. But for two thousand years the community of faith, identifying its Lord as the Servant of this passage, and identifying itself as with the transgressors, has lived in the light of an open promise too:

> Behold, I send the promise of my Father.

It's all we have; we join that hope.